AF413175

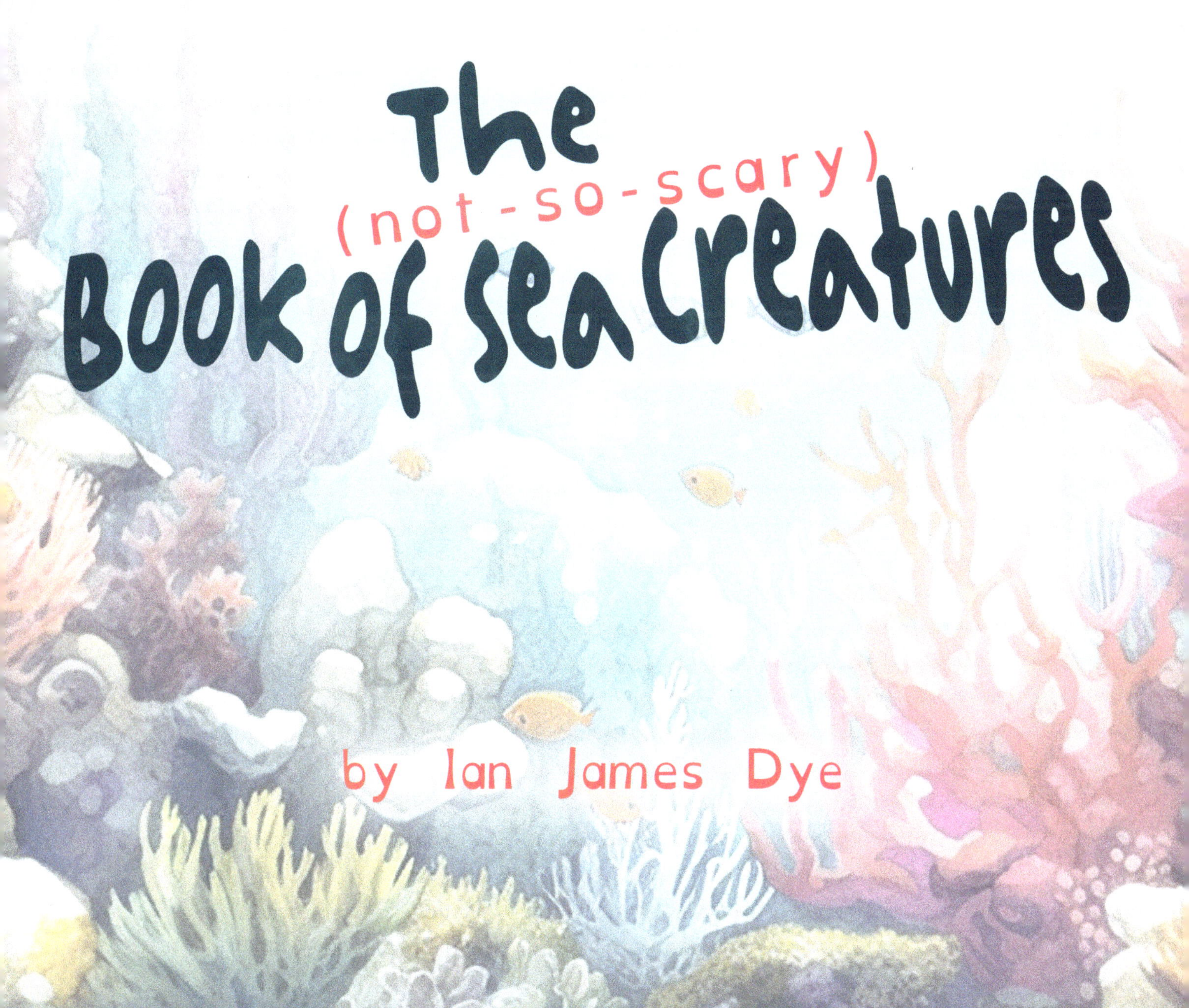

The
(not-so-scary)
BOOK of sea Creatures
by Ian James Dye

For D and J

Thank you for
always having the answer.

Some **JELLYFISH** are scary, but mostly they're okay,
They drift about the ocean, and slowly make their way.
They live throughout the water, both in cold and where it's warm,
If you see a bunch together, this is what we call a swarm.

This WHALE SHARK is so big and his mouth is 4 feet wide!
He opens up his jaws and sucks his food inside.
He's the biggest of the sharks, but also very slow,
He's just a gentle giant, but you would never know.

This creature's slow and clumsy and looks like a tasty dish,
Then he blows up like a ball because he's a **PUFFER FISH**
When he senses danger, he sucks the water in,
But then has trouble swimming as he tries to flap his fins.

This cutie is a **SEA OTTER**, he loves to swim and play.
He back floats on the water and relaxes most the day.
His flat tail helps with swimming and so do his webbed feet,
He uses rocks as tools to help him when he eats.

This creature is real sneaky and the hardest to contain,
This **OCTOPUS** is clever because she has 9 brains!
She can squish her body down to fit through holes and cracks,
And can blend into the background if a predator attacks.

This **MARLIN** is so fast and travels throughout the seas,
She leaps out of the water and darts around with ease.
Her snout is long and pointy and looks just like a spear,
But she only swings at fishes, so there's no need to fear.

This creature lives in rivers, in the bay and coastal seas,
Sometimes he's called a sea-cow, but he's a **MANATEE**
He loves to sleep and eat and his tail is very strong,
Although he's slow at swimming, he's in water all day long.

This **ORCA** isn't scary, although she's called a Killer Whale,
Her tail is 8 feet wide, but she's smaller than a male.
Her color is so pretty, she's mostly white and black,
But can you find her saddle? That's the gray patch on her back.

This creature has 2 claws that he can use to grab,
But he is not-so-scary, he's just a little CRAB
He spends his whole day hiding under rocks or in the sand,
Or maybe you can spot him walking sideways on the land.

This **STINGRAY** isn't scary, he's like a giant bat,
His tail is long and skinny and his body's wide and flat.
He digs in sandy bottoms, to find the food he needs,
And in the holes he makes, smaller fish will come to feed.

This creature's not-so-scary, she looks like you and me,
She dives under the water to learn about the sea.
She swims with fish and turtles and watches what they do,
Sometimes she may pretend that she's a fishy too.

This **SEAGULL** can drink water from the ocean and from lakes,
She can live all over Earth and eats whatever she can take.
She sleeps with one eye open to see when danger's near,
But if you drop a french fry, soon she will appear.

This BLOBFISH isn't ugly, he is handsome as can be,
And this is what he looks like while swimming in the sea.
He lays across the bottom with his mouth open wide,
In hopes that his food will find its way inside.

This creature's not-so-scary, she's just a cute **HARP SEAL**
She likes to dive and swim while looking for a meal.
She loves the icy water and rarely is on land,
When she calls out to her mother she can understand.

This creature's called a **SHRIMP**, his shell and tail are strong.
While **THIS** shrimp may be small, some are close to 1 foot long.
He sometimes will swim backwards with a flick of his strong tail,
Some make friends with fish and help them clean their scales.

This **BLUE WHALE** is so massive,
He's the largest that we know,
He's as long as 3 school buses,
That are lined up in a row.

His brain is also large,
Which means he's very smart,
But don't be scared of him,
Because he has a giant heart.

Though this **PENGUIN** is a bird, she can swim but she can't fly,
She spends half her life in water and none up in the sky.
She waddles on warm beaches or slides down ice and snow,
She lays eggs out of the water, but hunts for food below.

This **DOLPHIN** is so happy, she loves to swim and play,
She leaps out of the water and has a lot to say.
She lives with friends and family who also love to chat,
This dolphin's very smart, you can be sure of that.

This **CLOWNFISH** is so cute, she speaks with pops and clicks,
Some grow to be a few inches, but she's a whopping 6!
She lives in sea anemones, she feeds and cleans them too,
Sometimes she may come out by playing peek-a-boo!

I see a little **SEA STAR** but trust me he's not mean,
He can be different colors, some are orange and some are green.
He usually has **5** arms, but sometimes he has more,
He uses little feet to walk across the ocean floor.

This **WALRUS** is so big and he makes quite the splash,
But don't be scared of him or his large mustache.
His tusks look long and sharp, but still you shouldn't flee,
He hooks them on the ice to pull him from the sea.

This fish is called a **GROUPER** and her mouth is very big,
She uses it to eat and uses it to dig.
She sometimes can change colors to blend with the sea floor,
Look close and you might see her while swimming near the shore.

This **BELUGA WHALE** is friendly and she lives where it is cold,
She's gray when she is younger, then turns white as she gets old.
She has a group of friends and they can swim for miles,
Make sure to bring your camera, because she always has a smile.

This **PELICAN** is large and has a pouch in his long bill,
He scoops up salty water full of fish until it's filled.
You can spot him on a pier or on rocks right near the coast,
But don't be scared of him because it's fish he loves the most.

This creature is a SEA LION you can tell by her ear flaps,
They keep the water out while she's busy swimming laps.
She walks on all her flippers and can shout a mighty roar,
You might see her and her colony resting on the shore.

If you saw him in the sea, I wouldn't blame you if you hid,
But you have nothing to fear, he is just a **SQUID**
When he is afraid, he squirts a cloud of ink,
Then he jets away and is gone within a blink.

There are **7** types of **SEA TURTLE** that live for years and years,
They can hold their breath for hours, but there's no need to fear.
They're mostly in the sea and come on land to lay their eggs,
They look just like a tortoise but with flippers instead of legs.

This creature's called a SEAHORSE and she's actually a fish,
She clings to plants and changes to any color she may wish.
She does this when there's danger and makes sure that she's aware,
Of the creatures that swim past her and never know she's there.

This unicorn of the sea that your'e unlikely to meet,
Is actually a **NARWHAL** and his horn can grow 10 feet!
He lives in freezing waters and can dive down very deep,
But must remind himself to breathe, so he's never fully asleep.

This **GREAT WHITE SHARK** is scary, just look at those sharp teeth!
If one of them falls out, there's another tooth beneath.
His eyesight's very bad, but sense of smell is good,
But this shark is not-so-scary, he's just misunderstood.

Now that you've learned about the SEA
and CREATURES in this book,
Let's hop aboard the submarine
and take another look!

1. The numbers **1-10** are hiding in the pages, can you find them?

2. Can you find another creature in any of the pictures that is not named in the book?

3. Can you count how many arms the OCTOPUS has?

4. Can you count how many tusks the WALRUS has?

5. How many birds are in the book and can you name them?

6. How many creatures in the book live in cold areas?

7. Which sea creature is your favorite?